Felix Magg

Link between trade liberalisation and economic growth

Document Nr. V175634

Felix Magg

Link between trade liberalisation and economic growth

GRIN Verlag

Bibliografische Information der Deutschen Nationalbibliothek: Die Deutsche Bibliothek verzeichnet diese Publikation in der Deutschen Nationalbibliografie; detaillierte bibliografische Daten sind im Internet über http://dnb.d-nb.de/ abrufbar.

1. Auflage 2011

http://www.grin.com
Druck und Bindung: Books on Demand GmbH, Norderstedt Germany
ISBN 978-3-640-96676-9

Link between trade liberalisation and economic growth

Project

World Economy

Submission Date: 15 March 2011

Contents

List of figures

List of tables

1. Introduction

One of the great economic debates of all times is whether trade liberalisation or rather protectionism promotes economic growth (Case, Fair and Oster, 2009, p. 710). Ricardo (1955) claims with his theory of comparative advantage that specialisation and free trade benefits all participants. The producers and consumers ostensibly gain access to a wider range of products at lower prices and higher quality, the resources are used more efficiently, and the manufacturers may expand their products and facilities in foreign markets. However, in all times some politicians and market participants have been arguing against free trade and in favour of protection. Trade liberalisation would destroy jobs in non-competitve sectors, infant industries may have no chance to develop and the domestic economy depends to strong on foreign markets. The aim of this report is to discuss the link beween trade liberalisation and economic growth based on data and statistical outcomes.

2. Methodology

Before discussing whether trade liberalisation is effective in promoting economic growth, it is important to define what trade liberalisation actually is, and to justify what methods are used to do this. Without this it is not possible to judge whether it is effective or not. This report uses the index of restriction to trade and investment of the KOF Index of Globalization (Eidgenössische Technische Hochschule Zürich, 2011) to measure the level of trade liberalisation. The larger the value of this index the more liberalised the country is. Appendix A shows on which indices and variables this index is based as well as their weights and definitions. Economic growth is measured by the evolution of the GDP (Gross Domestic Product). Both variables, the index of restriction and the GDP, are available from 136 countries and six continents (Africa, Asia, Europe, North and South America, and Oceania) from 1970 to 2007. These data are analysed with the statistical programme SPSS to calculate several statistical outcomes (evolution, percentiles, correlation, and hypothesis test) in order to support the different arguments for and against trade liberalisation.

3. Evolution of restrictions and GDP

Figure 1 shows the evolution of the index of restriction to trade and investment in the six continents from 1970 to 2007. In all continents the restriction index increased over the 37 years, in particular since 1990. America, Asia and Oceania have currently nearly the same level of liberalisation. However, the restriction index of North and South America increased with on average 75.7% much faster than those of Asia and Oceania. Asia grew by 37.9% and Oceania only by 29.4%. Africa has the lowest level of liberalisation although it rose by 62.9%. Europe has, in contrast, the highest index but it increased only by 30.5%.

Figure 1: Evolution of the index of restriction

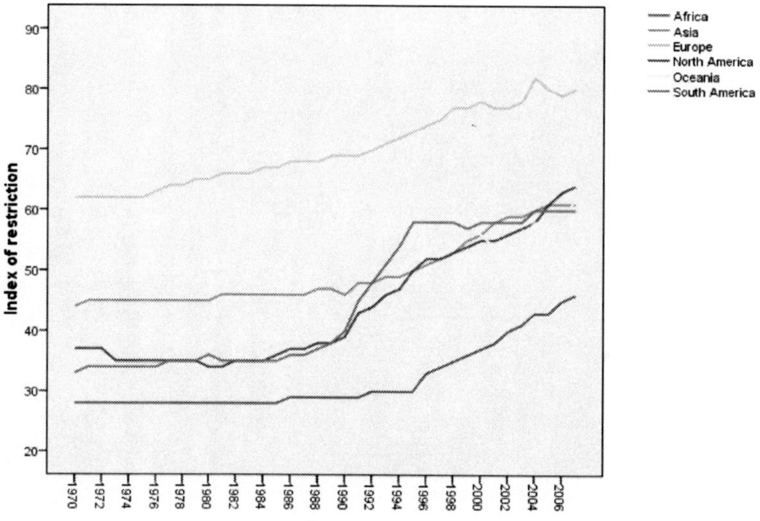

Figure 2 indicates the evolution of the GDP in billions of dollar. The GDP increased as well as the index of restriction in all continents. However, the distribution is much wider. South America had the highest increase with 245.4% while Europe had the lowest with only 54.5%. The GDP of the other continents grew all between 192.4 and 224.9% (see table 1). The highest level of GDP has currently North America followed by Asia and Europe. Asia overtook Europe in 1990. Oceania and South America are in the middle and Africa has the lowest level of GDP although it grew by 224.9%.

Figure 2: Evolution of the GDP

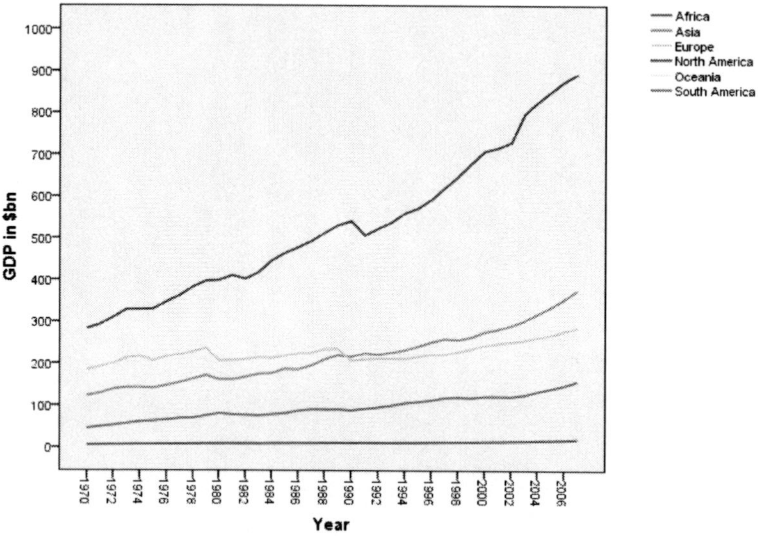

If both graphs are compared a clear relationship between the level of liberalisation and the growth of GDP can be seen. Those continents with the highest increase of liberalisation (North America, South America, and Africa) had the highest growth of GDP. In contrast, those continents with the lowest increase of liberalisation (Europe, Oceania, and Asia) had the lowest growth of GDP. Table 1 illustrates this positive relationship. However, this does not conclude that trade liberalisation supports economic growth. For example, despite the high level of liberalisation in Europe, the growth is at a low level, and the significant increase of liberalisation in South America in the 1990s did not lead to an equivalent growth in GDP.

Table 1: Evolution of restriction and GDP, 1970 - 2007

	Index of restriction
1. South America	+ 79.80%
2. North America	+ 71.52%
3. Africa	+ 62.94%
4. Asia	+ 37.94%
5. Europe	+ 30.50%
6. Oceania	+ 29.36%

	GDP
1. South America	+ 245.41%
2. Africa	+ 224.91%
3. North America	+ 215.59%
4. Asia	+ 206.17%
5. Oceania	+ 192.43%
6. Europe	+ 54.50%

4. Percentiles of the restriction variable

		Africa	Asia	Europe	North America	Oceania	South America
Mean		32.361703	50.193733	70.436483	44.294923	52.547526	45.255921
Std. Deviation		5.6078684	5.6341440	6.1751067	9.8713071	3.6666890	11.1212340
Minimum		28.2842	44.8286	62.0200	34.5607	48.6400	33.8640
Maximum		46.0875	61.8384	82.2216	64.4106	62.9200	60.8890
Percentiles	10	28.466333	45.739667	62.861767	35.250467	48.640000	34.519800
	25	28.479167	45.851667	65.123333	35.641333	49.733000	35.181000
	40	28.897611	46.512733	67.463267	37.538810	50.670400	36.113600
	50 (Median)	29.078194	46.957167	69.090000	38.370688	51.157000	38.443000
	60	30.297111	48.597290	70.873298	44.946000	51.769200	49.715600
	75	35.466389	54.336452	77.069211	54.033750	55.844000	58.484750
	90	43.237389	60.208871	79.284553	58.431875	58.396200	60.076400

Table 2: Percentiles of the restriction variable

The table above shows the percentiles of the variable of restriction to trade and investment in the six continents from 1970 to 2007. A percentile is a value of a variable that indicates the percent of a distribution that is equal or below to it (Darby and Goldfinch, 2007, pp 11-12). For example, the 10th percentile is the value equal or below which 10% of the observations may be found. The 50th percentile is the median which indicates the middle value in a data set. 50% of the observations will be above this point and 50% will be below this value (ibid., p. 11).

In the time from 1970 to 2007 Europe had the highest level of liberalisation. Its 90th percentile is 79.3. That means that only 10% of the values are above 79.3 and only 10% are under 62.9 as the 10th percentile is 62.9. The distribution is mainly equal. It ranges from 62 to 82.2. Africa had, in contrast, the lowest level of liberalisation over the 37 years. 40% of the values are under 28.9, only 10% are over 43.2, and the maximum is 46.1. Asia, North and South America and Oceania have nearly all a 90th percentile of 60. However, their distributions are different. Asia and Oceania has a relevant constant evolution. 10% of the restrictions levels are under 45.7 / 48.6 and over 60.2 / 58.4. In contrast the level of liberalisation in North and South America is very volatile. Their 10th percentiles are 35.3 and 35.5 whereas the 90th percentiles are 58.4 and 60. The standard deviations[1] confirm this. Oceania and Asia have a standard deviation of 3.7 and 5.6 while North and South America have one of 9.9 and 11.1.

The table also shows the minimum, maximum and mean of the variable of restriction from 1970 to 2007. They substantiate that Europe has the highest level of liberalisation as it has

[1] The standard deviation indicates how the data are clustered around the mean. A small standard deviation means data points are tightly bunched and a large standard deviation data points are spread apart. (Darby and Goldfinch, 2007, p. 10)

the highest mean as well as the highest minimum and maximum. Oceania has the second highest mean followed by Asia, South and North America. Africa has the lowest one. Nevertheless, the percentiles tell nothing about the relationship between liberalisation and economic growth. In order to analyse the link between liberalisation and economic growth the two variables have to set into correlation.

5. Correlation between level of restriction and GDP in the continents

In the tables in appendix B the correlation coefficient between the level of restriction and GDP for each of the six continents is indicated. In all continents the correlation between these two variables is very positive. The highest correlation has Oceania with 0.965. This means in 96.5% of the cases the GDP depends positively on the level of restriction. Figure 3 visualises the clear positive association in Oceania. The higher the level of liberalisation, the higher the GDP is. Europe has the lowest correlation with 0.79, however, still a clear positive relationship between liberalisation and GDP. All other continents have a very strong association of over 0.90.

Figure 3: Relation between restriction and GDP in Oceania

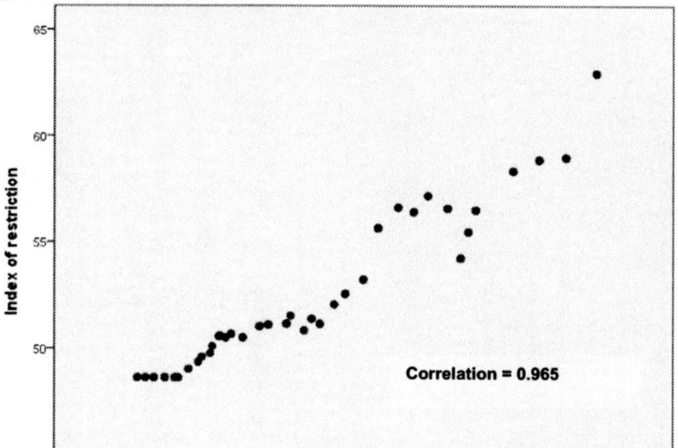

The significance of a relationship is measured by the sig (2-tailed) correlation coefficient. When it is less than 0.05 there is a significant linear relationship (Darby and Goldfinch, 2007, pp. 86-89). In all continents a significant correlation between liberalisation and GDP appears as the sig value is 0.000.

These results confirm the assumption at the beginning that there is a positive link between trade liberalisation and economic growth. There are three main reasons which explain the positive relationship. First, the consumers gain access to a greater variety of products at

lower prices and higher quality (Krueger, 1998; Gerber, 2005, p. 88-89). Relative expensive domestic products are replaced by cheaper products from countries which enjoy a comparative advantage[2] in the production of these products. Hence, the consumers have more money left to spend and to increase their welfare what is positive for the domestic economy. But also the trade partner benefits from free trade because its exports grow and it receives therefore more money.

Second, manufaturers could benefit from free trade because they gain as well as consumers access to cheaper and a wider range of inputs for their products (Thirlwall, 2000, p. 9). As a result, resources are used more efficiently as the move out of inefficient production (from industries with a comparative disadvantage) and into efficient production (to industries with a comparative advantage). Thus, the economy becomes more efficiently, i.e. it can produce more output for any given level of resources and technology. This greater efficiency increases eventually the rate of economic growth (Sawyer and Sprinkle, 2006, p. 48).

Third, domestic industries can expand their market and production into new countries (Thirlwall, 2000, p. 9; Gerber, 2005, p. 88-89). They might gain new customers around the wourld and could benefit from cheaper work forces from other countries. Thus, free trade has potential advantages for all market participants and all nations.

Nevertheless, an interesting question is why the correlation coefficient of Europe is so much lower than those of the other continents. The cause could be the convergence theory. The theory states that the growth rates of less developed countries will exceed the growth rates of developed countries due to the diminishing returns[3] (Case, Fair and Oster, 2009, p. 665). The trade liberalisation in the developed countries is already at such a high level that an increase of it has not such a big influence to the growth of GDP than it would have in developing countries. The industrialised countries have already reached their steady state.

6. Independent sample T-test (Hypothesis test)

In the previous paragraphs merely the correlation between trade liberalisation and growth of GDP of the six continents was considered. However, a positive correlation in one continent does not mean that there is a positive correlation in all countries. A further analysis indicates significant negative relationships in some countries, namely Burkina Faso, Democratic Republic of the Congo, Ethiopia, Kazakhstan, United Arab Emirates, Belize and Fiji and non-significant negative relationships in Lesotho, Georgia, Kyrgyz Republic, Russian Federation,

---

[2] Comparative advantage is "the advantage in the production of a good enjoyed by one country over another when that good can be produced at lower cost in terms of other goods than it could be in the other country" (Case, Fair and Oster, 2009, p. 699)

[3] The law of diminishing returns states that after a certain point, when additional units of a variable input (e.g. trade liberalisation) are added to fixed inputs (e.g. land), the marginal product of the variable input declines (ibid., p. 173).

Estonia, Ukraine and Papa New Guinea (see Appendix C). In all other countries the relationships are positive.

The correlations in DR Congo, Fiji and Ethiopia are with -0.861, -0.817 and -0.72 very negative. Figure 4 illustrates the negative relationship between trade liberalisation and economic growth in DR Congo. In years in which the liberalisation was very high, the GDP was very low whereas in years in which the liberalisation was low the GDP was relatively high.

Figure 4: Relation between restriction and GDP in Dem. Rep. Congo

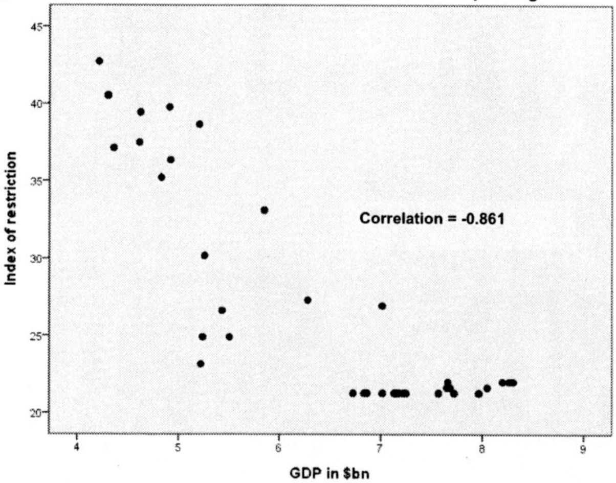

An important question is why these countries have a negative correlation and whether this alter the assumption that trade liberalisation is positively linked to economic growth. In order to answer this question a further look into to the spread of the index of restriction in the countries with a significant negative correlation compared to their continents with the help of the independent sample T-test is necessary.

In table 3 the restriction level of the Democratic Republic of the Congo is divided in two groups, one above and equals the median of the restriction index of the continent (Africa) and one below it. The table gives also information about the number of values (N), the mean and the standard deviation of both groups. Table 3 indicates a difference in the means in the two groups. However, this is only estimation. A hypothesis test is necessary to prove this assumption.

Table 4 summarises the test results and contains two hypothesis tests. The first is the Levene's Test for Equality of Variances. It checks whether the variances (spread) of the restriction index are approximately equal in the two groups. The hypotheses for the test are following:

H_0: Variances are equal

H_A: Variances are different

Since the sig value is less than 0.05 (see third column) the null-hypothesis (H_0) can be rejected with 95% confidence. Now the equality of means can be tested. The hypotheses are now:

H_0: Means are equal

H_A: Means are different

As the variances are different the second row of data ("Equal variances not assumed") is relevant. The sig (2-tailed) value is 0.00 (see row six) and hence the null-hypothesis can be rejected with 95% confidence. The means of the two groups are different. The result of both tests means that the average development of DR Congo's trade restriction differs from those in Africa. The other tables in appendix D show that also in all other countries with a significant negative correlation except of Burkina Faso and Ethiopia a distinction in the means appears. The independent sample T-test of Belize cannot be calculated because one of the groups is empty.

Table 3: Group Statistics Dem. Rep. Congo

Africa		N	Mean	Std. Deviation	Std. Error Mean
DR Congo	>= 29.0800	19	31.993684	7.0756273	1.6232602
	< 29.0800	19	21.423158	0.2801002	0.0642594

Table 4: Independent Samples Test Dem. Rep. Congo

		Levene's Test for Equality of Variances		t-test for Equality of Means						
									95% Confidence Interval of the Difference	
		F	Sig.	t	df	Sig. (2-tailed)	Mean Difference	Std. Error Difference	Lower	Upper
DR Congo	Equal variances assumed	95.918	0.000	6.507	36	0.000	10.5705263	1.6245316	7.2758234	13.8652292
	Equal variances not assumed			6.507	18.056	0.000	10.5705263	1.6245316	7.1582762	13.9827765

An important question is consequently why these countries diverge so much from all other ones. If the current situation in some of these countries is considered the causes are obviously. DR Congo is despite its immense economic resources one of the poorest countries in the world. Although its liberalisation index increased by 55.57% from 1970 to 2007 its GDP declined drastically by 13% (see Appendix E) due to the longstanding civil war and armed conflicts which cause a reduction of national output and government revenue, increased external debts, malnutrition and the deaths of more than five million people (BBC,

2010a). Thus, trade liberalisation was not able to cover the negative effectives of the civil war.

Although Papua New Guinea is richly endowed with natural resources, exploitation has always been a challenging prospect. High infrastructure costs and rugged terrain have made it difficult for Papua New Guinea to exploit natural resources to full potential. Human trafficking is another major problem. (Economy Watch, n.d.a).

The former Soviet Union states Russian Federation, Georgia, Estonia and Ukraine suffered due to the collapsing of the Soviet Union in the late 1980s and early 1990s and the difficulties which are caused by the transition from a planned economy to a market economy, such as high inflation, increased prices and unemployment (Case, Fair and Oster, 2009, p. 758-762) and hence the liberalisation did not lead immediately to an economic growth or the economy even decreased as in Ukraine. Georgia's economy suffered furthermore from the military conflicts in South Ossetia and Abkhazia in the early 1990s. (Economy Watch, n.d.b; BBC, 2010b). However, the negative correlation in the former Soviet Union countries is not signifanct as in the last years the economies have begun to recover and the liberalisation reforms are now effective. (World Bank, 2002, p. 4). Thus, in the long run the former Soviet Union countries benefit from trade liberalisation.

United Arab Emirates has been always a very open economy. In all 38 years its liberalisation index was at a high level of on average 88.4. Therefore, its economy has benefited from its open economy and the slightly fall of the liberalisation index by 8.8% from 1970 to 2007 has had no impact.

However, the other countries, Burkina Faso, Ethiopia, Lesotho, Kazakhstan, Kyrgyz Republic, Belize and Fiji, are exceptions. Although in all countries the liberalisation decreased over the last 38 years the GDP grew (see Appendix E). This fact contradicts the previous conclusion that trade liberalisation is positively linked to economic growth. Obviously there are also some negative aspects of trade liberalisation.

The main argument against free trade is that it would destroy jobs in non-competitive sectors (Case, Fair and Oster, 2009, p. 712). When, for example, the Europeans buy cheaper cars from China, the European carmaker sell less cars, make less profit and therefore might have to dismiss employees. However, the workers laid off in the contracting sector could be reemployed in expanding sector. In the developed countries, for instance, a transformation from labour-intensive industries to capital-intensive industry took place (Krueger, 1995). Hence, the resources are permanently used in the most efficient sectors - in the sectors having a comparative advantage.

Nevertheless, such a transformation causes always difficulties. The workers whose skills become obsolete have to learn new jobs which lead to additional expenditures for the economy (Case, Fair and Oster, 2009, p. 217). Furthermore, there is no guarantee that the new efficient industry will be able to employ all the labour thrown out of the closed inefficient industry (Thirlwall, 2000, p. 9). Generally, high-technology industries need fewer workers due to the increasing automatism. Thus, a complete specialisation is not optimal as it most likely leads to an increasing unemployment which has a negative effect on the economic growth. However, this does not conclude that trade protection is the most effective way to reach full employment; monetary, fiscal and labour market policies are often better ways (Gerber, 2005, pp. 138-139.).

Another argument for protectionism is that it would shield infant industries (ibid., p. 139). An infant industry is "a young industry that may need temporary protection from competition from the established industries of other countries to develop an acquired comparative advantage" (Case, Fair and Oster, 2009, p. 715). The argument is that if such an industry would not be protected it would never develop comparative advantage because the established industries can use the economies of scale[4] and other benefits they already have such as established customers or well endowed capital. The result would be that new domestic industries might have no chance to grow up which is negative for the economy as employment as well as competition in the domestic companies decreases.

Protection of infant industry is a common policy. For example in July 1991, the U.S. government imposed a 62.67% tariff on imports of flat-panel displays from Japan to protect the domestic laptop industry (ibid.). The consequence of such a protection is, however, that the advantages of free trade will be lost. The consumers have to pay higher prices and have a less choice of different products probably at lower quality. A further threat is that the producers could move their facilities abroad to avoid the tariff as the U.S. laptop producers did it (ibid.). Thus, such a protection policy may rather harm than benefit the economy.

A further disadvantage of trade liberalisation is the dependency on foreign markets. If exports have a significant part of a country's GDP the country depends very strong on foreign economies. Germany, which economy is very specialised in exports, is a good example. German manufacturers suffered very strong from the financial crisis as the demand in foreign countries declined rapidly and hence the exports fell too; in 2009 by 18.4% (Federal Statistical Office, 2010). Nevertheless, countries as Germany benefit very much in positive economic times. In 2010 Germany's exports grew by 18.5% (Federal Statistical Office, 2011a) and its economy by 3.6% (Federal Statistical Office, 2011b; BBC, 2011). Another country which is specialised in exports and benefited in the past very strong from trade

[4] The theory of economies of scale states that an increase in a firm's scale of production leads to lower average costs per unit produced (Case, Fair and Oster, 2009, p. 217)

liberalisation is China. China opened its economy very considerablely in the last 38 years. Its restriction index increased by 181.1% which helps the economy to grow by 2,354.9% from 1970 to 2007. Clearly, there is a positive relationship between trade liberalisation and economic growth as in figure 5 can be seen.

Figure 5: Relation between restriction and GDP in China

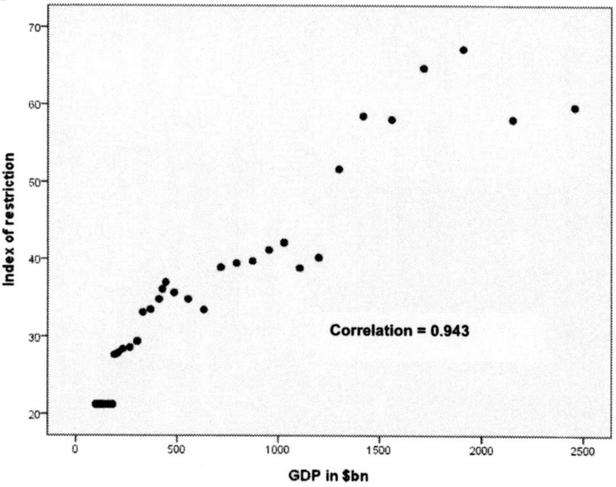

Hence, trade liberalisation does not guarantee economic growth. However, in the most countries arise positive correlations. Only in 14 of in total 136 countries appear a negative correlation and therefore the exceptions do not alter the previous conclusion that trade liberalisation promotes generally economic growth.

7. Caveat in the analysis

In all statistical calculations only the relationship between level of restriction and growth of GDP were regarded assuming that all other factors would be constant (ceteris paribus). However, this is not the case in the reality. A statistical correlation does not imply causality. There are a lot of further reasons for economic growth as well as decline which must take into account. Further reasons for economic growth could be, for example, an increase in labour supply, physical or human capital, or productivity (Case, Fair and Oster, 2009, p. 666). Reasons for economic decline could be a scarcity of capital, unability of capital accumulation, high inflation, capital flight[5], brain drain[6], corruption or social and political conflicts (ibid., p. 748-759). Further factors which might influence an economy both positive and negative are

[5] Capital flight is „the tendency of both human capital and financial capital to leave developing countries in search of higher expected rates of return elsewhere with less risk“ (Case, Fair, and Oster, 2009, p. 748)

[6] Brain drain is „the tendency for talented people from developing countries to become educated in a developed country and remain after graduation“. (ibid., p. 749)

the level of innovation, research and development, and entrepreneurship in a country, the amount of investment capital available, monetary and fiscal policy, and infrastructure (Stutz and Warf, 2007, pp. 380-381).

8. Conclusion

It is difficult to argue that there is a positive link between trade liberalisation and economic growth because there are some countries with negative correlations and trade liberalisation could lead to some disadvantages such as the loss of jobs in non-competitve sectors or the dependency on foreign markets. One the other hand the benefits are numerous: The market participants gain access to a wider range of products at lower prices and higher quality. The resources are used more efficiently and producers can expand their production. However, the positive correlations in most of the countries and the benefits of free trade indicate a positve causality between trade liberalisation and economic growth. In addition, other factors which could have influence on the economic development also have to be considered. It seems that trade liberalisation is a necessary, but not a sufficient, requirement for economic growth. In other words, openness alone cannot ensure that the economy growth, but without it, growth is unlikely to occur.

Reference list

BBC. (2010a). *Republic of Congo country profile.* [online] 30 Nov. Available at: <http://news.bbc.co.uk/1/hi/world/africa/country_profiles/1076794.stm> [Accessed 8 March 2011].

BBC. (2010b). *Georgia country profile.* [online] 1 Dec. Available at: <http://news.bbc.co.uk/1/hi/world/europe/country_profiles/1102477.stm> [Accessed 8 March 2011].

BBC. (2011). *German exports rose 18.5% in 2010.* [online] 9 Feb. Available at: <http://www.bbc.co.uk/news/business-12401835> [Accessed 3 March 2011].

Case, K., Fair, R. and Oster, S. (2009). *Principles of Economics.* 5th ed. London: Perason Prentice Hall.

Darby, P. and Goldfinch, J. (2007). *Introduction to SPSS 15.* Edinburgh Napier University, unpublished.

Economy Watch. (n.d.a). *Papua New Guinea Economy.* [online] Available at: <http://www.economywatch.com/world_economy/papua-new-guinea/> [Accessed 8 March 2011].

Economy Watch. (n.d.b). *Georgia Economy.* [online] Available at: <http://www.economywatch.com/world_economy/georgia/> [Accessed 8 March 2011].

Eidgenössische Technische Hochschule Zürich. (2011). *KOF Index of Globalization.* [online] Available at: <http://globalization.kof.ethz.ch/> [Accessed 6 March 2011].

Federal Statistical Office. (2010). *Germany's foreign trade 2009: export -18.4%; import -17.5%* . [online] Available at: <http://www.destatis.de/jetspeed/portal/cms/Sites/destatis/Internet/EN/Content/Statistics/Aussenhandel/Gesamtentwicklung/Aktuell.psml> [Accessed 8 March 2011].

Federal Statistical Office. (2011a). *German exports in 2010: +18.5% on 2009.* [online] 9 Feb. Available at: <http://www.destatis.de/jetspeed/portal/cms/Sites/destatis/Internet/EN/Content/Statistics/Aussenhandel/Gesamtentwicklung/Aktuell.psml> [Accessed 8 March 2011].

Federal Statistical Office. (2011b). *Gross domestic product (GDP).* [online] 9 Feb. Available at: <http://www.destatis.de/jetspeed/portal/cms/Sites/destatis/Internet/EN/Content/Statistics/VolkswirtschaftlicheGesamtrechnungen/Inlandsprodukt/Aktuell.psml> [Accessed 8 March 2011].

Gerber, J. (2005). *International Economics.* Boston: Pearson Addison-Wesley.

Krueger, A. (1998). Why Trade Liberalisation is Good for Growth. *The Economic Journal,* 108 (450), pp.1513-1522.

Ricardo, D. (1955). *The principles of political economy and taxation.* London: Dent.

Sawyer, W. C. and Sprinkle, R. L. (2006). *International Economics.* New Jersey: Pearson Prentice Hall.

Stutz, F. and Warf, B. (2007). *The World Economy.* 5th ed. New Jersey: Pearson Prentice Hall.

Thirlwall, A. (2000). Trade, Trade Liberalisation and Economic Growth: Theory and Evidence. *Economic Research Papers,* 63.

World Bank. (2002). *Transition: The First Ten Years – Analysis and Lessons for Eastern Europe and the Former Soviet Union.* Washington, DC.

Bibliography

Dreher, A. (2006). Does Globalization Affect Growth? Empirical Evidence from a new Index. *Applied Economics,* 38(10), pp. 1091-1110.

Parikh, A. and Stirbur, C. (2004). Relationship between Trade Liberalisation, Economic Growth and Trade Balance: An Econometric Investigation. *HWWA Discussion Paper,* 282.

Rodriguez, F. and Rodrik, D. (1999). Trade Policy and Economic Growth: A Skeptic's Guide to the Cross-National Evidence. *National Bureau of Economic Research (NBER),* 7081.

Winters, A. (2003). *Trade Liberalisation and Economic Performance: An Overview.* Brighton: University of Sussex.

Appendix A: Variables and weights of the restriction index

Indices and Variables	Weights	Definitions
Hidden Import Barriers	22%	The index is based on the Global Competitiveness Report's survey question: "In your country, tariff and non-tariff barriers significantly reduce the ability of imported goods to compete in the domestic market." The question's wording has varied slightly over the years.
Mean Tariff Rate	28%	As the mean tariff rate increases, countries are assigned lower ratings. The rating declines toward zero as the mean tariff rate approaches 50%.
Taxes on International Trade (percent of current revenue)	27%	Taxes on international trade include import duties, export duties, profits of export or import monopolies, exchange profits, and exchange taxes. Current revenue includes all revenue from taxes and nonrepayable receipts (other than grants) from the sale of land, intangible assets, government stocks, or fixed capital assets, or from capital transfers from nongovernmental sources. It also includes fines, fees, recoveries, inheritance taxes, and nonrecurrent levies on capital. Data are for central government and in percent of all current revenue.
Capital Account Restrictions	22%	Index based on two components: (i) Beginning with the year 2002, this sub-component is based on the question: "Foreign ownership of companies in your country is (1) rare, limited to minority stakes, and often prohibited in key sectors or (2) prevalent and encouraged". For earlier years, this sub-component was based on two questions about "Access of citizens to foreign capital markets and foreign access to domestic capital markets". (ii) Index based on the IMF's Annual Report on Exchange Arrangements and Exchange Restrictions, including 13 different types of capital controls. It is constructed by subtracting the number of restrictions from 13 and multiplying the result by 10.

Source: Eidgenössische Technische Hochschule Zürich, 2011

Appendix B: Correlations between index of restriction and GDP in the six continents

Correlations Africa

		Index of restriction	GDP
Index of restriction	Pearson Correlation	1.000	0.941**
	Sig. (2-tailed)		0.000
	N	38.000	38
GDP	Pearson Correlation	0.941**	1.000
	Sig. (2-tailed)	0.000	
	N	38	38.000

**. Correlation is significant at the 0.01 level (2-tailed).

Correlations Asia

		Index of restriction	GDP
Index of restriction	Pearson Correlation	1.000	0.948**
	Sig. (2-tailed)		0.000
	N	38.000	38
GDP	Pearson Correlation	0.948**	1.000
	Sig. (2-tailed)	0.000	
	N	38	38.000

**. Correlation is significant at the 0.01 level (2-tailed).

Correlations Europe

		Index of restriction	GDP
Index of restriction	Pearson Correlation	1.000	0.791**
	Sig. (2-tailed)		0.000
	N	38.000	38
GDP	Pearson Correlation	0.791**	1.000
	Sig. (2-tailed)	0.000	
	N	38	38.000

**. Correlation is significant at the 0.01 level (2-tailed).

Correlations North America

		Index of restriction	GDP
Index of restriction	Pearson Correlation	1.000	0.942**
	Sig. (2-tailed)		0.000
	N	38.000	38
GDP	Pearson Correlation	0.942**	1.000
	Sig. (2-tailed)	0.000	
	N	38	38.000

**. Correlation is significant at the 0.01 level (2-tailed).

Correlations Oceania

		Index of restriction	GDP
Index of restriction	Pearson Correlation	1.000	0.965**
	Sig. (2-tailed)		0.000
	N	38.000	38
GDP	Pearson Correlation	0.965**	1.000
	Sig. (2-tailed)	0.000	
	N	38	38.000

**. Correlation is significant at the 0.01 level (2-tailed).

Correlations South America

		Index of restriction	GDP
Index of restriction	Pearson Correlation	1.000	0.921**
	Sig. (2-tailed)		0.000
	N	38.000	38
GDP	Pearson Correlation	0.921**	1.000
	Sig. (2-tailed)	0.000	
	N	38	38.000

**. Correlation is significant at the 0.01 level (2-tailed).

Appendix C: Countries with negative correlation between index of restriction and GDP

Correlations Burkina Faso

		Index of restriction	GDP
Index of restriction	Pearson Correlation	1	-0.390*
	Sig. (2-tailed)		0.015
	N	38	38
GDP	Pearson Correlation	-0.390*	1
	Sig. (2-tailed)	0.015	
	N	38	38

*. Correlation is significant at the 0.05 level (2-tailed).

Correlations Georgia

		Index of restriction	GDP
Index of restriction	Pearson Correlation	1	-0.213
	Sig. (2-tailed)		0.200
	N	38	38
GDP	Pearson Correlation	-0.213	1
	Sig. (2-tailed)	0.200	
	N	38	38

Correlations Dem. Rep. Congo

		Index of restriction	GDP
Index of restriction	Pearson Correlation	1	-0.861**
	Sig. (2-tailed)		0.000
	N	38	38
GDP	Pearson Correlation	-0.861**	1
	Sig. (2-tailed)	0.000	
	N	38	38

**. Correlation is significant at the 0.01 level (2-tailed).

Correlations Kazakhstan

		Index of restriction	GDP
Index of restriction	Pearson Correlation	1	-0.599**
	Sig. (2-tailed)		.009
	N	38	18
GDP	Pearson Correlation	-0.599**	1
	Sig. (2-tailed)	0.009	
	N	18	18

**. Correlation is significant at the 0.01 level (2-tailed).

Correlations Ethiopia

		Index of restriction	GDP
Index of restriction	Pearson Correlation	1	-0.720**
	Sig. (2-tailed)		0.000
	N	38	27
GDP	Pearson Correlation	-0.720**	1
	Sig. (2-tailed)	0.000	
	N	27	27

**. Correlation is significant at the 0.01 level (2-tailed).

Correlations Kyrgyz Republic

		Index of restriction	GDP
Index of restriction	Pearson Correlation	1	-0.147
	Sig. (2-tailed)		0.513
	N	38	22
GDP	Pearson Correlation	-0.147	1
	Sig. (2-tailed)	0.513	
	N	22	22

Correlations Lesotho

		Index of restriction	GDP
Index of restriction	Pearson Correlation	1	-0.267
	Sig. (2-tailed)		0.255
	N	38	20
GDP	Pearson Correlation	-0.267	1
	Sig. (2-tailed)	0.255	
	N	20	20

Correlations Russian Federation

		Index of restriction	GDP
Index of restriction	Pearson Correlation	1	-0.464
	Sig. (2-tailed)		0.052
	N	18	18
GDP	Pearson Correlation	-0.464	1
	Sig. (2-tailed)	0.052	
	N	18	19

Correlations United Arab Emirates

		Index of restriction	GDP
Index of restriction	Pearson Correlation	1	-0.477**
	Sig. (2-tailed)		0.004
	N	38	35
GDP	Pearson Correlation	-0.477**	1
	Sig. (2-tailed)	0.004	
	N	35	35

**. Correlation is significant at the 0.01 level (2-tailed).

Correlations Fiji

		Index of restriction	GDP
Index of restriction	Pearson Correlation	1	-0.817**
	Sig. (2-tailed)	.	0.000
	N	38	38
GDP	Pearson Correlation	-0.817**	1
	Sig. (2-tailed)	0.000	
	N	38	38

**. Correlation is significant at the 0.01 level (2-tailed).

Correlations Estonia

		Index of restriction	GDP
Index of restriction	Pearson Correlation	1	-0.206
	Sig. (2-tailed)		0.428
	N	17	17
GDP	Pearson Correlation	-0.206	1
	Sig. (2-tailed)	0.428	
	N	17	28

Correlations Papua New Guinea

		Index of restriction	GDP
Index of restriction	Pearson Correlation	1	-0.316
	Sig. (2-tailed)		0.054
	N	38	38
GDP	Pearson Correlation	-0.316	1
	Sig. (2-tailed)	0.054	
	N	38	38

Correlations Ukraine

		Index of restriction	GDP
Index of restriction	Pearson Correlation	1	-0.203
	Sig. (2-tailed)		0.434
	N	17	17
GDP	Pearson Correlation	-0.203	1
	Sig. (2-tailed)	0.434	
	N	17	21

Correlations Belize

		Index of restriction	GDP
Index of restriction	Pearson Correlation	1	-0.596**
	Sig. (2-tailed)		0.007
	N	19	19
GDP	Pearson Correlation	-0.596**	1
	Sig. (2-tailed)	0.007	
	N	19	38

**. Correlation is significant at the 0.01 level (2-tailed).

Appendix D: Independent sample T-tests

Group Statistics African Countries

Africa		N	Mean	Std. Deviation	Std. Error Mean
Burkina Faso	>= 29.0800	19	54.4047	0.98345	0.22562
	< 29.0800	19	54.6300	0.00000	0.00000
DR Congo	>= 29.0800	19	31.993684	7.0756273	1.6232602
	< 29.0800	19	21.423158	0.2801002	0.0642594
Ethiopia	>= 29.0800	19	37.893158	1.1313809	0.2595566
	< 29.0800	19	38.270000	0.0000000	0.0000000

Independent Samples Test African Countries

		Levene's Test for Equality of Variances		t-test for Equality of Means						
									95% Confidence Interval of the Difference	
		F	Sig.	t	df	Sig. (2-tailed)	Mean Difference	Std. Error Difference	Lower	Upper
Burkina Faso	Equal variances assumed	7.490	0.010	-0.998	36	0.325	-0.22526	0.22562	-0.68284	0.23232
	Equal variances not assumed			-0.998	18.000	0.331	-0.22526	0.22562	-0.69927	0.24875
DR Congo	Equal variances assumed	95.918	0.000	6.507	36	0.000	10.5705263	1.6245316	7.2758234	13.8652292
	Equal variances not assumed			6.507	18.056	0.000	10.5705263	1.6245316	7.1582762	13.9827765
Ethiopia	Equal variances assumed	10.800	0.002	-1.452	36	0.155	-0.3768421	0.2595566	-0.9032473	0.1495631
	Equal variances not assumed			-1.452	18.000	0.164	-0.3768421	0.2595566	-0.9221503	0.1684660

Group Statistics Asian Countries

Asia		N	Mean	Std. Deviation	Std. Error Mean
Georgia	>= 46.9600	19	65.214211	3.1576350	.7244112
	< 46.9600	19	67.140000	0.0000000	0.0000000
Unit Arab Emirates	>= 46.9600	19	85.9695	1.45148	0.33299
	< 46.9600	19	90.9284	3.69006	0.84656

Independent Samples Test Asian Countries

		Levene's Test for Equality of Variances		t-test for Equality of Means						
									95% Confidence Interval of the Difference	
		F	Sig.	t	df	Sig. (2-tailed)	Mean Difference	Std. Error Difference	Lower	Upper
Georgia	Equal variances assumed	11.939	0.001	-2.658	36	0.012	-1.9257895	0.7244112	-3.3949634	-0.4566155
	Equal variances not assumed			-2.658	18.000	0.016	-1.9257895	0.7244112	-3.4477208	-0.4038581
United Arab Emirates	Equal variances assumed	20.667	0.000	-5.451	36	0.000	-4.95895	0.90970	-6.80389	-3.11400
	Equal variances not assumed			-5.451	23.440	0.000	-4.95895	0.90970	-6.83884	-3.07905

Group Statistics Oceania Countries

Oceania		N	Mean	Std. Deviation	Std. Error Mean
Fiji	>= 51.1570	19	33.214211	3.3108916	0.7595706
	< 51.1570	19	40.885789	2.3850817	0.5471753

Independent Samples Test Oceania Countries

		Levene's Test for Equality of Variances		t-test for Equality of Means						
									95% Confidence Interval of the Difference	
		F	Sig.	t	df	Sig. (2-tailed)	Mean Difference	Std. Error Difference	Lower	Upper
Fiji	Equal variances assumed	6.986	0.012	-8.195	36	0.000	-7.6715789	0.9361348	-9.5701483	-5.7730096
	Equal variances not assumed			-8.195	32.718	0.000	-7.6715789	0.9361348	-9.5767828	-5.7663751

Group Statistics North American Countries

North America		N	Mean	Std. Deviation	Std. Error Mean
Belize	>= 38.3700	19	33.708947	2.8321505	0.6497399
	< 38.3700	0[a]	.	.	.

a. t cannot be computed because at least one of the groups is empty.

Appendix E: Evolution of the index of restriction and the GDP in countries with negative correlations, 1970 - 2007

Country	Evolution of the index of restriction	Evolution of GDP	Significance
Congo	+ 55.57%	- 13.06%	sig.
Papua New Guinea	+ 63.06%	+ 158.41%	not sig.
Georgia	+ 61.36%	+ 13.26%	not sig.
Russian Federation	+ 27.02%	+ 3.19%	not sig.
Estonia	+ 8.94%	+ 98.51%	not sig.
Ukraine	+ 40.82%	- 27.38%	not sig.
United Arab Emirates	- 8.88%	+ 504.18%	sig.
Burkina Faso	- 7.05%	+ 381.82%	sig.
Ethiopia	- 9.96%	+ 168.17%	sig.
Lesotho	- 3.21%	+ 81.11%	not sig.
Kazakhstan	- 20.12%	+ 37.06%	sig.
Kyrgyz Republic	- 7.05%	+ 14.03%	not sig.
Belize	- 23.18%	+ 700.35%	sig.
Fiji	- 15.3%	+ 166.42%	sig.

Lightning Source UK Ltd.
Milton Keynes UK
UKOW05f2237190813

215623UK00001B/212/P

9 783640 966769